Cool Breezes: No Dogs Allowed
The Story of the West Beach Corporation

Lee's Rocks, Beverly Farms

Front cover: 1911 pavilion, burned 1948
Back cover: 1949 bathhouse, "small" bathhouse dating to 1900

Cool Breezes: No Dogs Allowed
The Story of the West Beach Corporation

Edward R. Brown

and

Frank R. DiPaolo, Jr.

Beverly Historical Society
Beverly, Massachusetts

First Printing: 2015

ISBN 978-1-891906-11-4

Beverly Historical Society
117 Cabot Street
Beverly, MA 01915

www.beverlyhistory.org

Ordering Information: Special discounts are available on quantity purchases by corporations, associations, educators, and others. For details, contact the publisher at the above listed address.

U.S. trade bookstores and wholesalers: Please contact Beverly Historical Society, 978-922-1186; or email info@beverlyhistory.org

Contents

Foreword 1

Way Back When: The Beach and the Farms 4

Founding the West Beach Corporation 13

The Early Years: Seaweed Supply to Bathing Beach 18

The Misery Island Connection 32

Disaster Years: 1948 and 1978 37

Celebrating the Fourth of July 44

Surviving a Bitter Challenge 50

The West Beach Corporation Today 56

Appendix: Presidents of the Corporation 60

Foreword

The idea for writing a history of West Beach originated with Beverly Historical Society volunteer Frank DiPaolo, who discussed it with various members of the West Beach Corporation Board of Directors. With their encouragement, Frank began to assemble some materials and enlisted the assistance of fellow Society volunteer Ed Brown. They continued and expanded their research and plans for a small book. Early in 2007, health issues forced the late Frank DiPaolo to cut back on his activities, at which time Ed Brown offered to finish the work they had started.

The history of West Beach can be documented to the 17th century. The West Beach Corporation, which owns and maintains the property for the benefit of its members and subscribers, is a rather unique non-profit corporation, in existence for more than a century and a half. It is governed by four officers and a seven-member Board of Directors, who are elected annually in October by the membership using a paper ballot. The corporation was formed by the Great and General Court of Massachusetts under Chapter 157 of the Legislative Acts of 1852. Although the main focus of beach property use has changed drastically, from collection of seaweed as fertilizer by farmers in the mid-19th century, to summertime recreation by the 1890s and onward, the corporation has continued to function in much the same way since its founding. At present, from Memorial Day weekend until Labor Day, the beach property is dedicated to the exclusive use of Beverly Farms residents, certain other beach members and their guests. At other times the public is welcome, with certain restrictions. One of those restrictions is a sign reading "No Dogs Year Round," which suggested part of the title for this book.

All expenses of operating and maintaining the property, including after-hours security, are the responsibility of the corporation, not Beverly taxpayers. Much of the funding comes from the annual sale of beach stickers (even voting members and other Beverly Farms residents must pay to park, and even then a space is not guaranteed), along with locker rentals. It should be pointed out that even though some maps show "West Beach" as including more than a half mile of shoreline, only about 650 feet of beachfront is owned by the West Beach Corporation. All of the remaining stretch of sand is privately held by individual property owners. And, contrary to popular belief, the West Beach Corporation is not the sponsor of the annual Fourth of July fireworks display. The holiday celebration and its funding are the responsibility of the Farms/Prides Fourth of July Committee. For many years, the beach directors have made the premises available for the holiday activities as a community gesture. After successfully fighting a challenge to the corporation's 140-year-old tax exempt status in the early 1990s, negotiations led to an agreement for West Beach to make an annual payment to the City of Beverly under terms of the PILOT program (Payment In Lieu Of Taxes).

Two earlier documents on West Beach history have been written, neither of which were formally published. In 1936, Elsie P. Doane of Beverly Farms, a descendant of original beach proprietor John West, composed a typed 14-page paper, which she titled "West Beach, Beverly Farms, Mass." About 1999, researcher and historian Allen Hovey of "Search Werks" compiled a 20-page document entitled "Beverly's West Beach and the West Beach Corporation." That work was written largely to refute the claims of a group of persons dedicated to the goal of seizing control of the beach and opening it up to all residents of Beverly. That process even led to creation of an elected "charter commission," the efforts of which were happily rebuffed thanks to the work of the West Beach board and its legal team, strongly supported by opinions and rulings of the state Attorney General, the Beverly City Council, and a Superior Court judge. The authors have used both of those papers as reference materials, along with a number of other published sources. With the frequent changing of clerks over the years, the corporation has not maintained central archives. And with our space limitations, we have not attempted a "complete" history of the beach, choosing instead to focus on highlights over the years.

A disclaimer here: The authors are not "neutral observers." Although we have striven for historical accuracy throughout, both of us have ties to the West Beach Corporation, and for many years have been numbered among its supporters. One is a long-time member of the corporation (never an office-holder), and was even employed there a half century ago; the other was a subscriber. Any errors or omissions in this paper are entirely the responsibility of the authors, and nothing herein should be taken to reflect the official positions of the West Beach Corporation, its officers or directors.

A trivia note: A check on the Internet revealed that there is another West Beach Corporation in the good old U.S.A., out on the "left coast." That West Beach Corporation is a commercial venture located at 60 North Venice Boulevard, Venice, California 90291. At least at that distance there is little chance for the two corporations to be confused.

We dedicate this work to old John West and his son Thomas; to the founders of the corporation; to everyone who has given time, talent and money over the years to make sure that the goals of the founders have been maintained; and to all who have enjoyed West Beach.

Edward R. Brown

Frank R. DiPaolo, Jr.

In "pre-history," that is, before the coming of the first English settlers, the area of what is now West Beach and its surroundings was in the territory of the Agawam Indians. The Agawams and their neighbors to the south, the Naumkeags, were peace-loving people who appear to have lived by farming, hunting, and perhaps fishing. When they first arrived here is uncertain. We do not, of course, know what the shoreline looked like at the start of the 17th century and before. It is apparent that the Agawams held property in common, and one of their favorite summer camping places may have been around the former Haven estate, now the area of 45 West St.

Sometime around 1616-17, large numbers of native Americans in Eastern Massachusetts were wiped out in a plague, most likely a disease introduced by European traders and to which the Indians had no natural immunity. Only scattered bands remained when Roger Conant and the first permanent settlers of Salem arrived in 1626 and were soon joined by many other colonists. Those few Indians welcomed the English and sought their protection against raids by more warlike tribes to the north, notably the Tarrantines.

In 1680, Humphrey Woodbury, one of the first settlers of Beverly, gave his recollections of what relations with the surviving Agawams and Naumkeags were like: "\

> When we settled, the Indians never molested us, in our improvement (of the land) or settling down, either at Salem or Beverly sides of the ferry, but showed themselves very glad of our company, and came and planted by us, and often times came to us for shelter, saying they were afraid of their Indians up in the country, and we did shelter them when they fled to us, and we had free leave to build and plant where we have taken up lands.

Masconomet, the Sagamore (chief) of the Agawams, would sell the territory of Ipswich (including what is now Hamilton and Essex) to John Winthrop Jr., son the founding governor of the Massachusetts Bay Colony, who also resided at Ryal Side until 1645. Masconomet, who became a Christian, died in 1658 and is buried on Sagamore Hill in Hamilton. When he and several other chiefs including the Squaw Sachem of Naumkeag converted to Christianity in 1643, they were told that they would have to observe the Sabbath by refraining from any work. The sagamore's answer, according to the early colonial records, was that since their depleted state left them little to do any day, resting on Sunday was no problem. In 1700, three grandsons of Masconomet, Sam English, Joseph English and John Umpee, brought a claim on all the territory of Beverly, Wenham and other towns on the grounds that the old chief's sale to Winthrop had included only Ipswich. The colonists took them seriously enough to purchase a "quit claim" through the county court.

All of what is now Beverly, Manchester, Wenham, Danvers, Topsfield and Marblehead was part of the original town of Salem. The first white owner of the land surrounding West Beach was not the legendary John West, but John Blackleach. According to Sidney Perley, who published a three-volume *History of Salem* in the 1920s, on Feb. 16, 1635-36 the town of Salem granted 300 acres to Blackleach (see map). The hyphenated date is explained by the fact that until 1752, England still used the Julian calendar, which had March 25 as the first day of the year, long after the rest of Europe had adopted the reformed Gregorian calendar. James Savage, the 19th century compiler of colonial genealogies, wrote that Blackleach came to Salem in 1634 and took

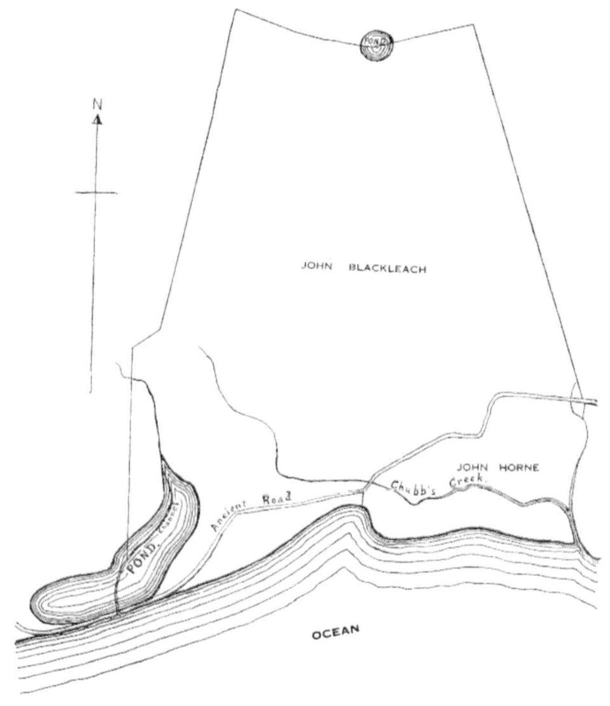

the oath of freeman on May 6, 1635. Savage describes him as an "active merchant" who represented Salem at the General Court in 1636, and with his wife Elizabeth had six children baptized in the Salem Church. He would be the first to receive a land grant at what is now Beverly Farms, but he never lived there. When he moved to Boston he at first leased, and then sold, his 300 acres to John West. West did in fact move with his family to the former Blackleach grant. A map of Beverly as it appeared at the time it separated from Salem in 1668, published by Sidney Perley, shows that there were then only three houses in what is now Beverly Farms. West's home was located by the road near what is now Lee's Crossing.

Nicholas Woodbury lived at the "headland" south of West Beach, and the third house was farmer Jeffrey Thissell's, which still stands at 574 Hale Street. Back then, much of the territory of Beverly Farms was considered "common" land. Besides West's two parcels (see map) and the Woodbury and Thissell lots, there were only four other privately owned parcels here, including a stretch of marshlands toward Manchester originally granted to John Horne, later conveyed to William Pitt and Moses Maverick. They may have used it to harvest salt marsh hay.

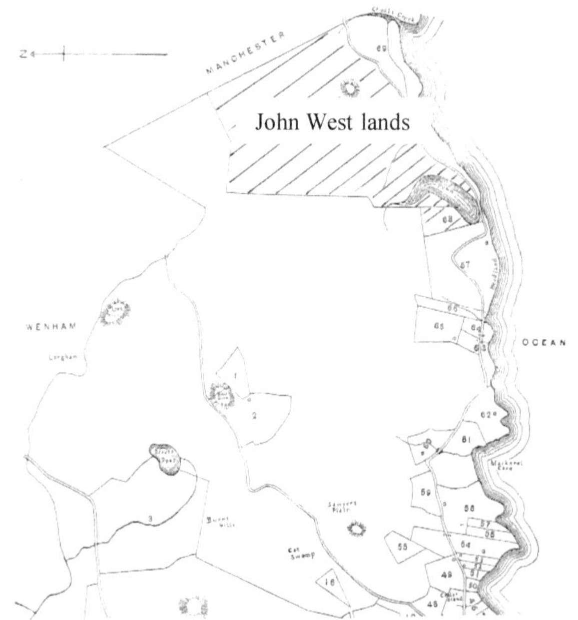

It is apparent that some of the land surrounding West's property, including the beach itself, was at first considered "common." But that all changed on Feb. 12, 1666-67. On that day, as related in Vol. 2, p. 394 of Perley's history, the selectmen of Salem "agreed with John West 'at the Creek' that while he should maintain 'the Causeway over the marsh at the farm which was Mr.

Blackleech's in Salem bounds a sufficient highway to the town of Gloucester and the Manchester men's use; he shall enjoy the use and benefit of all such ground as lieth in Common, between the said farm and the farm of Nicholas Woodbery with pond and beach; and hath liberty to set up a gate thereon for his use.'

This causeway is on West Street, near Hale street, at Beverly Farms." (The last sentence is Perley's addition.)

From that day, West Beach – at least the part of it fronting West's land, which includes the present corporation's stretch of seashore – clearly became private property. And when 21 months later Beverly was allowed to break away from Salem to become a separate town, all of the previous Salem land grants stood good. The property passed to West's heirs, then to proprietors. As we shall see, by the mid-1850s, disputes regarding proprietorship would lead to formation of the West Beach Corporation by the residents of Beverly Farms through an 1852 act of the state legislature. That was done at the suggestion of the selectmen of Beverly and with approval of the town meeting. The grant to John West mentioned a "pond" as well as the beach. Early maps show the presence of a large fresh water pond, sometimes known as Long Pond or Blackleach's Pond, just inland from the ocean. In fact, it extended so close to the seashore that it was just barely possible to locate a road between the beach and pond. In 1696, a storm surge broke through the fragile barrier and caused the pond to drain into the sea, never to refill. That event washed out the road and caused a flurry of communications between Beverly and Manchester, which were now all but cut off from each other. A Manchester town meeting on Oct. 19, 1696, complained that "the country highway that was lately laid out within the precincts of the town of Beverly on the beach namely West's Beach being broken up by reason of the pond breaking into the sea ....makes that part of the way very hazardable and difficult for travelers." That reference makes it clear that "West's Beach" was a commonly used name before 1700. The towns agreed to cooperate in rectifying the situation. Beverly picked a committee of Andrew Elliott, Paul Thorndike, William Raymond and Samuel Corning. Those four met on March 19, 1697 with Manchester representatives John Siblee, Robert Leach, Samuel Allen Sr. and John Ley, at which time they agreed on a new highway which would run from the causeway near what was then the home of Thomas West (John's son and heir), running across West's land and the Common north of Cornelius Larcom's land, across Benjamin Woodberry's pasture till it finally rejoined the old road "at a white pine tree marked on two sides...." (Essex Institute Historical Records (EIHC), Vol. 20, p. 211). Because of the expense involved in building a new road, the highway surveyors of all four Beverly "squadrons" were directed to "warn out" all their men to share the work in equal proportion. That's how highways were built in those days, with every able-bodied man expected to contribute his share. The Beverly town meeting vote also refers to "the breaking out of the pond into the sea at the long beach between our town and Manchester commonly known by the name of farmer West's Beach, which occasions the laying out of a new way from Plum Cove to farmer West's land." Today, houses and railroad tracks occupy the space that once was a large pond. It's interesting to speculate that given the proximity of the pond to the beach, adventurous Farms children in the 17th century who wanted to cool off on a summer afternoon would have had the choice of either fresh or salt water.

John West, by the way, was a man held in high regard by his fellow citizens. When Beverly held its first town meeting in November of 1668, John West was one of five men elected to the important office of selectmen, chosen, as Edwin Stone wrote in his 1843 History of Beverly, "from among the most worthy of the citizens." And in 1679, according to Stone, "John West presented a flagon to the church, as a token of his love." That was then Beverly's only church, the First Parish, of which the Rev. John Hale was pastor.

The origin of the name West Beach is easy to trace. But just when "Beverly Farms" came into general use as the title of the neighborhood is more difficult to determine. As early as 1713, the town of Beverly granted some land "to the Farms, on which to erect a schoolhouse." (Frederick A, Ober article in *History of Essex County*, 1888, vol. 1, p 695.) "The Farms" is not defined, nor is the location of the land given. We can only surmise that the citizens of the outlying area wanted a school for their children, presumably built at their own expense. We don't know whether the school was actually built. We can be sure that by the 1820s a distinct village had emerged, centered around the present intersection of Hart and Hale streets. There was the newly built church; Perry's store at the current front of the church parking lot, a general store where the stage coach to Gloucester stopped and horses were watered at the trough which stands to this day; a school, probably one room; and perhaps a couple of small shops. And certainly by that time "Beverly Farms" had come into general use. The Essex County history previously cited includes this note: "1829 – at the Farms this year a church was organized, and the Rev. Benjamin Knight ordained pastor Sept. 2nd.

It started as a 'Christian' church, but afterwards became, under the leadership of Mr. Knight, united with the Baptist denomination in 1834." The church building may date to 1825, and was built using bricks from the former first cotton mill in America; this was replaced in 1844 by the familiar wooden edifice.

The first written mention of Beverly Farms found so far is in 1831, when the "parent" First Church in Beverly presented a communion flagon engraved "to the Church at Beverly Farms" (Stone's *History of Beverly*). Going by that, we can be sure that Beverly Farms had become the accepted name before that time. By the time the Gloucester Branch of the Eastern Railroad was built in 1847, Katherine Peabody Loring, late president of the Beverly Historical Society wrote in 1932, "Beverly Farms was already an established name." But the first station here, located near the present Lee's Crossing, was called "West Beach." In the 1850s, a Beverly Farms business district centered on West Street was starting to take shape.

The railroad built a new station at the present location about 1859 and renamed it Beverly Farms. After the Boston & Maine acquired the Eastern, it built the new depot, part of which still exists, in 1898. By the middle of the 19th century, the Farms had two school districts. The East Farms school was located in the "Hollow" near present 752 Hale Street; the West Farms school was near Indian Hill. In 1873 the two districts were consolidated into one Beverly Farms School on Haskell Street at Webster Avenue. The Beverly Farms Cemetery was established in 1840.

Beverly Farms had an independent post office by 1877 and probably earlier, since that is the oldest directory available at the Beverly Historical Society. It was located then on Oak Street, opposite the train station, making it easy to load and unload outgoing and incoming mail. By 1897 it had moved to Hale Street near the Farms Square, with Lawrence J. Watson as postmaster. Mail came in and went out twice in the morning and twice in the afternoon, much better service than we get today. The post office then relocated to the Neighbor's Hall block at 8 West Street, before ending up further down on West Street.

Not much is known about West Beach in the years between the West family ownership and the establishment of the corporation. But we can insert a couple of interesting notes. With the outbreak of the Revolutionary War, residents of the coastal towns, including Beverly, feared attack by ships of His Majesty's Navy. Vol. 43 of the EIHC (1907) includes an article, "The seacoast defenses of Essex County in 1776." That year, a committee was named to examine the state of coastal defense between Boston and Newburyport.

Part of their report reads as follows:

> At Beverly they have erected a sand bank battery laid out for five Ambozears in which they have two borrowed field pieces. This battery appeared to the committee of no great importance. The situation of a seven gun battery nearly opposite Salem Fort, in Woodbury's Point and a four gun battery erecting on Thorndick's Point together with a five gun battery erected at Barnett's Point and a three gun battery at West Beach are of such a nature as to demand an immediate attention for the preservation & security of the sea coast.

"Salem Fort" would have been Winter Island, and "ambozears" undoubtedly meant embrasures, openings for gun barrels. Thanks to Nancy Coffey, we have excerpts from a lecture delivered in 1831 by Robert Rantoul Sr., one of Beverly's leading citizens of the time. Rantoul certainly took the "long view" in describing West Beach, which he said that "from Josiah Ober's house at the western end it extends easterly toward Manchester about a mile." He gives us a clue that the Revolutionary War battery was in fact at the Prides end of the stretch of sand, near Josiah Ober's, since "very near this farmhouse there is a high hill which rises very abruptly, where, in the Revolutionary War, a battery was erected." Mr. Rantoul, later in his 1831 lecture, remarked that "the coarse sand from West's beach and some other beaches is an article of trade that has employed several vessels in transportation to Boston where it is used with lime in composition of mortar for laying of bricks and plastering the inside of buildings." And with the establishment of the first church in the Farms, West Beach became the site for baptisms, and these weren't conducted in the summer months. Mrs. Loring, in her 1932 article, tells us that the 1820s church "at first was called simply Christian, but in a few years became Baptist and even until comparatively late years the members were baptized by total immersion at West Beach in the month of October." B-r-r-r! But it could have been worse. They could have picked January.

Over the years there were two initiatives by residents of Beverly Farms to break away from Beverly. In his paper "Beverly in 1700" (EIHC, vol. 56, 1920), Sidney Perley referred to a "slight attempt" in 1717 to have the remote eastern part of Beverly joined to Manchester. At a Manchester town meeting June 3, 1717 (we have cleaned up the spelling of the Manchester clerk, which was atrocious even for that time), it was "voted to choose a man to send to the General Court with the men of the farm of Captain West of Beverly with a petition to get them off from Beverly," and also that "Capt. John Knowlton is chosen to go with such gentlemen of Captain West's farm as they shall appoint to go to the General Court with a petition for their getting off from Beverly to us at Manchester." Nothing came of this. No reason was given, but it can be taken as a matter of convenience, since Manchester's meeting house was barely two miles away, while Beverly's was more than double the distance.

Much more serious was the effort in 1885-1888 by both "townies" and summer residents to break away from Beverly and become a proposed separate town of Beverly Farms. Many reasons were advanced, including disproportionately high property assessments, lack of municipal services, and separation of the village from Beverly proper. The town would have included about all of the present Ward 6. To complicate matters, the few families of the far eastern tip of Wenham known as "Little Comfort" wanted in, too, which provoked opposition from land-starved Wenham. The "divisionists" came within an eyelash of success in 1887, when both houses of the legislature passed the bill to create the new town. But the celebration in the Farms was silenced when Governor Oliver Ames vetoed the bill, and since the margin of passage had been less than two-thirds, the veto stuck. Beverly Farms was one signature away from being a town, but lacking that signature it would remain forever part of Beverly. Another division bill in 1888 went down to defeat. Just a few years later, Beverly changed from town government to a city charter, in part so there could be no future attempts by dissatisfied Farms folks to break away.

Founding the West Beach Corporation

At its beginning, the West Beach Corporation was all about the seaweed. Farmers living near the seashore prized the rockweed and kelp which washed ashore with the tide as a favored fertilizer for their crop-bearing fields. If it hadn't been for squabbles over that seaweed, the corporation never would have come to pass in 1852. Certainly old John West must have been delighted in 1666 to obtain his own private stretch of beach, with all of the rich bounty God provided him whenever storm waves stirred up the ocean floor.

John West died Oct. 6, 1683 at the age of 68, without leaving a will. His oldest and only surviving son, Thomas (born in 1642) was appointed administrator of his father's estate. John West and his first wife Mary had three sons, but Joseph died in 1660 at age 16, and John passed away in 1668 at 21. Thomas West brought an inventory of his father's estate to the November 1683 session of the Salem Quarterly Court. That inventory, compiled by Beverly residents Paul Thorndike, William Rayment and Samuel Leach, had a total value of about 529 pounds English money, of which housing and lands totaled 400 pounds, with the farm animals – cattle, swine, horses and sheep – adding up to 83 pounds, and his farm implements, tools and household goods accounting for the rest. John West, despite his service to the town as selectman and representative to the General Court, could not read or write as shown by the fact that both he and his second wife Mary (Ley) signed with a mark a document in 1680 that gave Mary all the right to her late husband Henry Ley's estate, in return for her waiving all right to John West's estate if he predeceased her.

Thomas West inherited his father's farm along with West Beach, and lived there for the rest of his life. He was the "Captain West" who along with his neighbors approached Manchester in 1717 with the idea of having their remote corner of Beverly "set off" to Manchester. According to the notes of researcher Beverly C. Carlman, Thomas West and his first wife Elizabeth (Jackson) had nine children born between 1663 and 1683, of whom six survived to maturity. (Daughter Mary married Robert Woodbury in 1698, and the old house at 824

Hale St. was built for them.) After Elizabeth died, the captain married Sarah Cook in 1710. His military title refers to his rank in the town militia; he was not a seaman. His occupation was given as "yeoman," meaning farmer. Thomas West lived to what was a very ripe old age for that time of 80 or 81, dying on March 28, 1723.

Trying to trace the ownership of West Beach after the time of Capt. Thomas West would be too time consuming for the scope of this work. The name of West continues to appear in Beverly records well into the 19th century. Certainly, the original 300 acre farm soon began to be carved up into smaller pieces, both from legacies to succeeding generations and ensuing private sales. According to Beverly Carlman's hand-written notes in the possession of the Beverly Historical Society, Captain West's youngest son, Thomas, lived at what is now 914 Hale Street after he married Christian Woodbury in 1702. Writing in her 1936 paper on West Beach, Elsie P. Doane, herself a descendant of John West, noted that 15 other Farms residents of that time – with the last names of Larcom, Mayberry, Davis and Preston – shared the same ancestral distinction. What we can be sure of is that by the early 1800s, the last of the Wests were gone from the vicinity of the beach that bears the family name. Left on the scene, however, were a number of residents who claimed access to the beach as "proprietors" in the right of John and Thomas West.

That meant, in addition to "fowling" (hunting ducks and other shorebirds), the right to load up their horse-drawn carts with a share of that bountiful seaweed and haul it home to nourish their crops. But as the village of Beverly Farms continued to grow by the 1840s, disputes among the locals over those "proprietorship" rights were becoming more and more vocal. Since there were no newspapers or police blotters to turn to, we don't know whether those disputes ever became physical. Apparent also is that at least a few "outsiders" attracted to the still open beach were trying to slip in and grab a share of the seaweed bounty. But by mid-century, the people of Beverly Farms were tired of the squabbling and were ready to seek a sanctioned way of settling things on a permanent basis. They would take their case to the Beverly Town Meeting, a gathering of all the town's legal voters (men only, of course, in those days).

The June 7, 1851 issue of the recently established Beverly Citizen weekly newspaper included a warrant for a town meeting to be held at the Town Hall on Thursday, June 12, at 1 p.m. The meeting was to act on six articles, with Article 5 reading as follows: "To see if the town will take measures to ascertain the rights of individuals and of the public in West Beach, West Causeway and West Street, as far as the public travel and the interests of the town may seem to require." No newspaper report of the town meeting exists, but it can be inferred that the issue was far too complex for the voters to spend a lot of time debating. But in the town records, the town clerk made the following entry regarding Article 5: "Voted, that the fifth article in the warrant be referred to the Selectmen, with instructions to take such measures in regard to West Beach, West Causeway and West Street as the interests of the town, and the public travel may seem to them to require." It was all very straightforward; nothing underhanded there.

The selectmen – Joseph E. Ober (surprisingly, a Beverly Farms man), William E. Lovett and Haskett D. Whitney – after debating the matter and checking the historical record, came up with a novel solution that would, with state legislative approval, allow the aggrieved men of the Farms to forever determine the future use of the beach. The selectmen's order reads in part that they were: "...fully persuaded that the rights of proprietorship in said Beach, are founded at most entirely on the writing or obligation so called given to John West, the 19th of February 1666, by the town of Salem in consideration of his maintaining the causeway, the same standing now on the Salem records and nothing showing to the contrary...that same has ever been annulled, the selectmen would recommend to the proprietors and all interested that they form themselves into a corporate body according to law, with a view of petitioning the legislature the ensuing winter for an act of incorporation."

Armed with this favorable directive from Beverly's top town officials, the men of Beverly Farms wasted no time in following up. A mass meeting must have been called, almost certainly at the Baptist church on Hart Street. Allen Hovey, in his 1999 analysis *Beverly's West Beach and the West Beach Corporation*, points out that in 1850 Beverly Farms consisted of 150 families and a total population of 690, and that the 102 adult males who adopted and signed the West Beach incorporation petition "constituted the entire voting male segment of the village."

To make sure that nobody with any claim to rights in what would be a village association would be excluded, the meeting agreed that beach rights would be offered to all residents of the East Farms school district, along with those residing in that part of the West Farms district "as far west as William Perry's house."

No resident would be required to join the corporation, but those who did would be expected to bear their portion of expenses and would "receive their proportion of whatever benefits may accrue." Peter Pride, a 60-year-old farmer, was the first of the 102 men to sign the petition seeking incorporation, which was dated October 20, 1851, and was then submitted to both houses of the Massachusetts legislature. It concluded with these words: "We therefore pray that we may become a body politic for the purpose of holding and improving said proprietary, according to the original purpose of the said grant." To make sure that their point of origin was clear, the petitioners described themselves as "citizens of that portion of the town of Beverly in the County of Essex, known as Beverly Farms."

Farming and shoemaking were the primary occupations of Beverly Farms residents in 1851. It was decidedly a village of working class people. It would be another 20 years before the first of the wealthy "summer people" would start to show up, and when they did, they would not patronize West Beach. Those "colonists" would organize their own exclusive enclaves, such as the Myopia Hunt Club, Essex County Club, and the Prides Beach Association. West Beach was at the beginning, and has continued to be, a playground for those who live on "the other side of the tracks."

From all we can gather, there was no move to oppose the petition when it came before the legislature. On Feb. 21, 1852, the Massachusetts Senate passed a resolution supporting "An Act to Incorporate West's Beach Corporation." On the following day, the House of Representatives followed suit. The resolution stipulated that the petitioners present a copy of their petition to the Beverly town clerk, publish it in both the Salem Register and the Beverly Citizen, and that it be ratified at Beverly's annual town meeting that March. The petition was published on Feb. 28, in time for the March 8 town meeting. At that gathering the Beverly voters gave their approval on the motion of leading citizen Robert Rantoul, after adding an amendment suggested by E. Pousland, Esq. that the proprietors of the beach continue to be responsible for maintaining "the causeway near said Beach, and also the road adjoining upon said Beach." With the imprimatur of the town in place, formal approval of the new corporation followed quickly. What would be officially known as Chapter 157 of the Acts of 1852 was signed into law by Governor George S. Boutwell on April 28, 1852. The West Beach Corporation was now official.

Acting quickly, Peter Pride on behalf of others named in the Act of Incorporation posted a public notice for an organizational meeting to be held Monday, June 28, 1852 at 7:30 p.m. "in the Chapel of the Second Baptist Society." The agenda included choice of a moderator, approval of the act of incorporation, choice of a clerk, election of officers and adoption of bylaws, plus the regulation for calling future meetings. It would in reality be the nearest thing Beverly Farms would ever have to a town meeting. The church on Hart Street was next to the Farms general store, Perry & Haskell, goods and groceries, commonly called "Perry's Store." (Later known as the "Pump Cottage," it burned to the ground in November 1947.)

Those present decided that "the officers for this corporation be balloted for at once and on one piece of paper." That paper ballot procedure continues to this day. At an adjourned session on July 18, Joseph E. Ober was chosen the first West Beach president; Samuel A. Edwards as both clerk and treasurer. The five directors included Mr. Ober, Benjamin Preston, Alvin Haskell, David Larcom, and Thomas Preston 2nd. No wealthy Brahmins are included there. The West Beach Corporation was in business to stay.

Although some maps of Beverly show "West Beach" as occupying half a mile of shoreline, that is a false indication. John West never owned more than the stretch of sand that fronted on his farm. And when the West Beach Corporation came into existence in 1852, its boundaries were clearly defined. The beach corporation controlled only 650 feet of shoreline at the high water mark, and that is all it owns today. A map drawn by Allen Hovey in 1995, based upon the reading of Chapter 157 as adopted in 1852, shows that the corporation property was bounded by West Street, the land of Jonathan Preston (now 97 West St.), and land of the heirs of James Woodberry (now set off by a high stone wall). The approximate low water mark encompassed the familiar ledge then known as Cove Rocks. Mr. Hovey included that drawing in his West Beach analysis. By comparison, Mr. Hovey notes that Beverly's public Dane Street Beach at Lyons Park contains, in addition to seven acres of grassland, some 1,500 feet of beachfront.

The West Beach Corporation came into existence at a time when Beverly Farms was on the verge of change. One of the catalysts for change was the construction of the Eastern Railroad's branch line from Beverly Junction to Gloucester, passing through the heart of Beverly Farms. The first train ran in 1847. The line was given the name Gloucester Branch, because the extension to Rockport did not occur until 1861. The clatter of the stagecoach was replaced by the chuffing, clanking and shrieking of the fire-breathing 4-4-0 wood burners that pulled the trains in the years before either Westinghouse air brakes or automatic couplers were invented. (Children must have been thrilled to see the railroad arrive.) An old map published by Joseph Garland in his book *The North Shore* reveals that an early proposal for the route of the branch would have taken it about two miles inland from its eventual route, passing through near the present location of Route 128 and missing the Farms almost entirely. Fortunately for the village that route was not adopted, or its later history might have been quite different. Woodberry Page, the stagecoach driver who lost his situation when the trains arrived, landed nicely on his feet, securing a position as station agent at Beverly. The railroad not only opened the way for more development and increased population, it also opened new vistas for the locals. Travel became easier and more convenient, and although commuting wasn't a common option at first, the train made it possible for someone to live in one town and hold a job in another. Delivery of goods also became much faster. Materials that had to be delivered laboriously by horse-drawn wagon over questionable roads could now be carried by freight car to a siding and freight house right in town. The track passed in sight of West Beach, so riders traveling through could see the possibilities the village had to offer. The first station, in fact was located near what became known as Lee's Crossing, and actually bore the name "West Beach." About 1859 it was moved to its present location and renamed Beverly Farms. Certainly over the ensuing years the railroad brought many new residents to town, all prospective members of the corporation.

Included in the act of incorporation of West Beach was a requirement that the association construct a wall to separate its property from the public way known as West Street. After organizing by election of officers and directors, the corporation wasted no time in fulfilling that task. Less than eight months later, in a letter dated Beverly Farms, March 4, 1853, the directors of the "West's Beach Corporation" invited the selectmen of Beverly to examine the wall. Four days later, Beverly Town Clerk Samuel A. Edwards returned a certified copy signed by all five selectmen stating that: "Agreeable to the above request of the Directors of West's Beach Corporation we have examined the wall referred to ...and hereby signify our concurrence with said Directors as to their having complied with so much of said 'Act' as relates to building a wall alongside said beach." Elsie P. Doane pointed out that both letters contain the signatures of the same man – Joseph E. Ober as beach director and as Beverly selectman.

The beach corporation also assumed the responsibility originally given to John West in 1666, of maintaining the causeway or stone bridge that carried West Street over Chubb's Creek on the way to Manchester, a road originally laid out in 1646 by Thomas Lothrop, Salem founder Roger Conant, William Woodbury, Richard Brackenbury, Laurence Leach and William Dixey. In 1867, the beach directors ordered that "all legal voters included as members of said corporation shall be liable to a uniform assessment of one dollar and twenty-five cents each and such further expenditure as may be necessary to keep the wall and causeway in good repair..." Anyone delinquent in paying this assessment would lose all privileges until the deficiency was made good. From all we know, the beach continued that responsibility until the Commonwealth of Massachusetts designated West Street and parts of Hale Street as a state highway (Route 127). At that time, the state took over maintenance of the roadway and causeway, but the corporation remains responsible for the wall.

But in the 1850s, the main interest for members of the new corporation was preserving and protecting rights to harvest seaweed. When bylaws were adopted, Articles 4 and 5 dealt with what was then the greatest asset the beach provided.

"Article 4 – In regard to carrying seaweed from the beach or landing, the following rates shall be observed. Every member of the corporation shall pay into the treasury of this corporation for each load of seaweed drawn by one horse 2 cents, one pair of oxen 4 cents, and in the same proportion for all additional teams."

"Article 5 – No person shall gather upon or remove seaweed or any other material from the premises of this corporation upon the Sabbath day under a penalty of ten dollars for each offense." (In other words, the fine for patronizing the beach on Sunday was worth the value of 500 loads of seaweed taken out on any other day.)

But the rules for removal of seaweed fertilizer seemed to work very well, and put an end to the previous squabbling. In their very first annual report to the membership, dated March 1853, the West Beach directors put it in colorful terms: "Your directors feel that in order to receive the full benefits of the Act of Incorporation, the act itself as well as the bylaws of the corporation must be adhered to by its members. They think that already they can discover in the community benefits that have resulted from the movement. We have made and consummated – we have not infrequently – heard it observed within the past few months that we are not obliged to now as formerly go to the beach long before high water, and watch the seaweed in the water with the vigilance of a hawk watching his prey, lest our neighbors should come in before us and set up a prior claim while the stuff is surging up and down in the surf, just because he happened to have legs a little longer than our own, thus at once cultivating a wish or to say the least a very selfish feeling. So far as we know, individuals who make the greatest use of the seaweed appear to have their quantum and are satisfied." (Elsie P. Doane, p. 7.)

To understand how the beach operated in the 1850s and 1860s, we have to realize that in those days the concept of "leisure" was almost completely unknown. People worked from sunrise to sunset six days a week, and Sunday was reserved for rest, contemplation, and attendance at two public worship services.

The thought that someone might want to go to the beach just to lie around, to soak up the sun and cool off in the waves would have been shocking. Even children, when not in school, were expected to contribute their efforts to the family's financial well being. Youngsters had their games, sports and outings when they could get away with them. More than likely, a few adventurous boys might strip on a hot summer afternoon for a brief cooling frolic in the surf if they could be sure their elders and sisters weren't watching, before hurrying home to their chores in time to avoid a licking. In the days of the one-room schoolhouse, school "kept" whenever a teacher was available. If two or three district schools in a town shared one teacher (as Wenham town records reveal), one might operate for four or six months, then close in favor of another. Modern educational "reformers" who would like to deprive children of their cherished summer freedom in favor of year-round classes keep repeating the myth that the current school year is an obsolete product of the "agricultural economy." In fact, the reverse is true. For years, Harvard College held its commencement in August, not June. The modern school calendar developed in the mid to late 19th century when rural villages gave way to towns, towns became cities, the grade promotion system was adopted, and one or two-room schoolhouses were replaced by multi-room "grammar" schools. (Beverly Farms didn't get a "modern" school until 1873, when the old East and West Farms districts were combined into one central building on Haskell Street.) Since it was realized that children could not be kept at their lessons without a break, and because the large school buildings became infernally hot in the summer, officials decided it made sense to shut down for July and August.

As the 19th century moved into its latter decades, changes would come to West Beach, entirely transforming the corporation's mode of doing business. One by one, the farms of the "Farms" disappeared as their owners chose to go into other lines of business, or moved inland to towns with more plentiful space and more fertile ground. New houses and streets replaced what had been farmland. The seaweed that was once so prized now became a liability, as it piled up on the beach with no "takers." By 1887, it became necessary to get the membership involved in cleaning the seashore. Every West Beach member had to either contribute a day's work when called upon by the directors to help clean the beach, or pay a two dollar assessment so someone could be hired in their place. In 1899, the $75 cost of hiring men and teams to remove seaweed and rubbish was such a burden that the directors thought it might be better to permanently employ one man. For a while, George Lee gave permission for the corporation to dump seaweed on his land located on the opposite side of West Street; later an arrangement was made with two farmers from Peabody who still cherished seaweed to haul the beach "supply" away, "thereby saving the corporation quite a sum of money,' as Elsie P. Doane put it.

But the winds of a true "sea change" began to blow by the start of the 1880s. The dawn to dusk work ethic that so drove our ancestors didn't disappear overnight, but for the first time people began to see the need for a bit of fun, the benefits of adding some healthful relaxation to their lives. After the Boston, Revere Beach and Lynn Railroad began its narrow gauge steam operations in 1875, city folk now had easy access to the wide stretches of Revere Beach. That soon became a favored destination for day trippers who wanted to get away to the cool seaside. "Bathing costumes" for men and women (a far cry from today's bathing suits) made their appearance in the fashionable department stores. Beverly Farms and its Prides Crossing adjunct had by the 1880s started to attract the rich and famous, who built their summer palaces as getaways from the heat of city life. While they weren't patrons of West Beach, their lifestyle wasn't entirely overlooked by the less affluent residents, many of whom built the mansion houses and worked on the grounds. Knowing that Beverly Farms had its own little stretch of splendid seashore that was in essence the property of the entire village, people here began to see the beach as a place they could go to cool off, to admire the ocean view, and to meet their friends. Slowly but surely, by the 1890s the 650 feet of sand with its cooling ocean breezes had become a cherished part of summer for many residents of Beverly Farms. With school out of session, mothers could take their children to the beach, and even Dad might be able to join them for an hour or two in the late afternoon. Those who had the means could even go for a row in the harbor. The Naumkeag Directory reveals that by 1897, the members of the Hannable family were operating a boat rental business on the West Beach property, obviously with the approval of the corporation directors. That boat rental livery did not disappear from the directory until 1921. As the old song says, "By the sea, by the sea, by the beautiful sea..."

We should also point out that during World War I, the patriotic directors of the West Beach Corporation offered use of the premises to the U.S. government for military purposes. When the U.S. entered the war in the spring of 1917, there was concern about the havoc being caused in the Atlantic by German submarines, known as U-boats (for Undersea). Writing on May 10, 1917 to Godfrey Lowell Cabot of Beverly Farms, who had assumed command of the First Naval Reserve Camp in Marblehead, West Beach Clerk William R. Brooks composed this letter:

"At a meeting of the Directors of the West Beach Corporation, it was voted that we offer the U.S. Government through Lt. G. L. Cabot, the use of two large rooms, gent's toilet, corridor and lookout of the Pavilion and grounds west of the Pavilion free of rent, the U.S. Government to pay for any changes that may be necessary. The vote was unanimous."

Replying two days later, Cabot, the aviator who had flown his seaplane from Misery Island, said he did "highly appreciate your patriotic offer which has been communicated to the Commandant of the First Naval District.

I will let you know as soon as I have his answer." The Navy decided it did not need the West Beach lookout, but at least the offer was made.

Godfrey Lowell Cabot

Pier, Bathhouses and Rules for Access

In the early years of the West Beach Corporation there is no evidence that any structures stood on the property. Some early records speak of a "landing," which apparently was a spot reserved to launch or land boats, and to position carts for the loading of seaweed. A meeting of the corporation in 1885 mandated that the Board of Directors post notices regarding the removal of seaweed and sand "at the upper and lower entrances to the beach." A detailed 1880 map in the possession of the Beverly Historical Society shows two small buildings on the premises of the "West's Beach Corp." Both of those shacks were located on what would be the dry sand, not far from the boundary of the Jonathan Preston property that is now 97 West St. What those structures were used for is unknown. That same map indicates that there were three short entrances from West Street to the beach property – one close to Preston's bounds, one near the center, and a third almost at the far end.

By the time the next detailed map was published in 1897, use of the beach had evolved to a recreational facility, and the map reflects that change. A long row of small buildings, labeled "Bath Houses," appears on the map. Some of those actually are shown to be on the adjacent private beach of the "J. Preston Heirs," which is possibly an erroneous placement by the map maker, since the corporation property for some reason is divided into two lots, and none of the structures are on the right hand portion. It is possible, of course, that the Preston family did erect bathhouses on its section of beachfront for private rental. The next map, published ten years later in 1907, still shows the structures on the Preston beach, but it also stretches a dozen bath houses across the corporation's waterfront. Tucked away against the high stone wall that separates West Beach from the 143 West St. driveway is a row of tiny sheds that could be the storage facility for the Hannable boat rental concession, which we know was in business by that time.

Pictorial evidence exists for those 1897-1907 bath houses, better known as the "beach shacks." An undated photo from a postcard (below) in the files of the Beverly Historical Society, which must have been taken about 1905, shows a mismatched line of about 12 wooden structures jammed close together, some with pitched roofs, others flat, many sporting covered porches facing the water. On a sign atop the building at the far left, the words “To Let” can be made out.

Two or three gaggles of beach-goers, female and male, dressed in outfits that left little skin exposed, are strolling about or sitting on the sand.

At the far right can be seen a very familiar sight, a stuccoed building with four windows along the wall. It’s the West Beach “small bathhouse,” looking much as it does more than a century later. This building also appears on the 1907 map. According to Elsie P. Doane, the small bathhouse was purchased from “Messrs. Lee and Tweed,” who must have been the builders. For years it was uncertain whether those “beach shacks” were owned by the corporation or, judging from their haphazard architecture, were erected by individual beach members for use by their own families. But the chance discovery of a brief item in the June 9, 1906 edition of the Manchester-based *North Shore Breeze* throws considerable light on the subject. Under the Beverly Farms Notes, the unidentified correspondent informed readers: “The Board of Directors of the West Beach Corporation have (sic.) recently purchased the bath houses at West Beach, heretofore owned by Messrs. Publicover Bros., which now brings to the corporation complete control of all bath houses used for commercial purposes.”

There's a wealth of information crammed into that single sentence. We now know that the row of beach shacks was in fact a private enterprise of a Beverly Farms construction firm. According to the Beverly City Directory for 1903, Publicover Bros., carpenters and builders, had a shop on Hale Street near West Street (Beverly Farms Square), "3 doors from A. O. Marshall's Store," as their display ad proclaimed. (Marshall's was the drug store at 1 West St., which had the Marshall's Hall meeting place upstairs.) Brothers John M. and Willard B. Publicover were prominent Farms residents. John lived near the shop, and Willard, one of the founders of St. John's Episcopal Church, had a home on Hart Street near Greenwood Avenue. The tone of the brief news item makes it clear that the carpenter shop brothers had built the beach shacks (obviously with approval of the Board of Directors), then rented them out by the season for their own profit. As proved by the 1897 map, the structures went up in the 1890s when people were taking more interest in leisure time activities, spurred perhaps by the excitement over the 1893 World's Fair. Obviously, beach-goers now were willing to pay to have a place where they could change into their "bathing costumes," keep a beach umbrella handy to shade them from the sun's rays, and sit on their own small private veranda if the day was too hot for the sand. By 1906, the corporation obviously wanted to assume complete control, so the Publicover interests were bought out. In just a few years, the beach shacks would be only a memory, replaced by something much better. Also, the words "complete control of all bath houses" makes clear that the familiar structure at the east end of the property, with its four attached entry ways and now known as the small bathhouse, was corporation property after its construction by Lee & Tweed.

For almost eight decades, one of the most popular features of West Beach was the long pier that extended into the ocean just to the east of Cove Rocks. Its wooden pilings were driven deep into the sand, its deck provided a promenade with a fine view, and at low tide those seeking shade could stake out a spot "under the boardwalk," as the Drifters' hit song from the summer of 1964 put it. The high diving board provided a challenging rite of passage for physically fit children, who usually jumped feet first into the deep water while holding their noses, and an opportunity for teens and young adults who wished to show off their form as "real" divers. You could fish from the end of the pier, usually with indifferent results, and on the Fourth of July it was the place where set pieces were mounted for the fireworks display, with the aerial rockets ignited at the far end. A postcard photo of the pier taken in the first decade of the 20th century has the scrawled message of a young visitor to Beverly Farms who spent a day at West Beach: "Where we went swimming. Had a slick time. Stayed in all day."

The Pier circa 1920

Until 1938, the pier also boasted an extension, a walkway ladder and substantial dock where boats could be landed and tied up. The pier was constructed on the corporation property in 1900, when its use as a landing place was vitally important to a new enterprise on Misery Island. (We will examine the "Misery Island connection" in greater detail later.) Early that year, the offshore island that is a prominent view from the shore of West Beach was sold, along with its small uninhabitable neighbor, Little Misery, to a group of Boston investors who had big plans to turn the bigger island into a private summer resort. A clubhouse and a nine-hole golf course were quickly constructed, among other amenities. Since the sandy cove that provided the island's only safe landing place faced directly toward West Beach, the syndicate that ran the Misery Island Club realized that was the best place for the steam launch that would operate to and from the island to tie up while it dropped off and picked up guests and their baggage, along with essential supplies and materials. Corporation records show that the Misery Island Club paid about 20 percent of the cost for the Beverly Farms firm of Hardy & Day to erect the pier, with the rest paid through public subscription and a loan. The West Beach Corporation allowed the club to use the pier that was so vital to the island resort in its all-too-brief existence. They and their successors would benefit for a few years, but the beach would benefit far more until a memorable storm made the pier disappear.

Although the corporation owned the beach shacks starting with the summer of 1906, it wouldn't be long until they were banished. Not only was the row of buildings unsightly, it made access to the sand difficult and also posed a fire risk, since if one of them ever caught fire, the flames would quickly spread to all the others. In 1910, the directors decided to dispose of those bath houses to anyone who would move them, and demolish any that had no takers. In their place was a vision for a grand pavilion that would be the pride not only of West Beach but of this entire section of the North Shore. One of the former beach shacks ended up on Oak Street, as the office for the Connolly Brothers construction firm. Elsie P. Doane wrote in 1936 that "In some people's back yards you may see a one room building usually with wide doors and a piazza. Those are the beach houses moved to the owner's property when the pavilion was built." By "owners" she undoubtedly meant the folks who for a long time had leased the structures, first from the Publicover Bros. and then from the corporation, and were given the right of first refusal at dispersal time in the fall of 1910. Despite their haphazard appearance, Mrs. Doane remembered that "we had mighty good times there."

With the seaside vista cleared of the beach houses, in 1911 the firm of Hardy & Day was chosen to build the grand pavilion. Messrs. Hardy & Day must have employed all their workers on the project, which took shape quickly that spring. To those who recall the original West Beach pavilion, it was a place of wonder. It included 224 private locker rooms (large enough for two people to occupy at once), toilet and shower facilities, a first aid room and superintendent's office, a concession stand, a long covered veranda where elders could sit in the shade or beach-goers could escape a sudden shower – it was plenty big enough, too, for band concerts – and children loved to climb to the upstairs lookout from which they could see everything that was going on along the beach and spy on their friends. The pavilion was topped off by a magnificent flagpole, from which Old Glory proudly waved every day the beach was open. There was even a blackboard on which the day's water temperature and the time of high tide were posted.

According to *Beverly Times* correspondent Joseph M. Donovan, writing on July 17, 1948, the pavilion was financed through a subscription drive, and even the wealthy summer people were solicited, though they did not use the beach. Records show that several gave, including $1,000 from Henry Clay Frick. The cost for Hardy & Day to construct the pavilion was $18,000. But with 224 lockers available for rent, the West Beach Corporation now had a ready source of cash, to pay the construction debt and the expanding cost of operating the beach. People loved the convenience of having a locker room where they could change out of a wet bathing suit and store all their beach gear for the entire season. Suddenly, West Beach was a mini-resort for the people of Beverly Farms.

Construction of the pavilion coincided with another "sea change." It was about that time that the automobile was gaining in popularity. Not only could those able to afford the gasoline powered transportation offered by Henry Ford and other car manufacturers show off their new acquisitions around town, they also could load up the family and take off on sight-seeing tours. Now West Beach had to offer parking facilities to members, and it also had to put in place some security measures to guarantee that, reminiscent of the 1851 "seaweed wars," outsiders didn't swarm in to hog both parking spaces and the beach itself. With the buildings (two bathhouses) to maintain, cleanup and maintenance to perform daily, policing of admission and the safety of patrons, it would be necessary for West Beach to have paid summer staff for the first time. This started with just a superintendent, helped by a few corporate volunteers, but it soon became necessary to expand the paid crew to include young assistants and a lifeguard. A job at West Beach became a sought-after prize for college students home for the summer. They wouldn't get rich, but they could work by the seaside and check out the local "talent."

As the number of cars expanded, a sticker system was put in place to make sure those entering the premises had a right to be there. For many years the stickers were free, first to members of the corporation and then to all eligible residents of Beverly Farms. In later years, as the budget shot up, even residents had to pay an annual sticker fee. Also, when people moved out of Beverly Farms to surrounding communities (this often happened when young couples got married), they missed their beloved beach and wanted to keep the privileges they had enjoyed. The directors moved to accommodate them by establishing a seasonal but non-voting membership category called "subscriber." Those accepted into that limited category – there soon would be a waiting list – were allowed to purchase parking stickers and to rent lockers – if available – at a higher rate than residents paid. Helping to police the rules was the fact that no parking was allowed on the state highway, and local streets around the beach also were posted for no parking. Until the 1960s there was a "walk-in" gate through the West Street wall, but after complaints that it was being used too much by non-members being dropped off there, the gate was walled in and pedestrians had to enter through the drive-in gate. Farms children literally grew up at the beach during their long summer vacations, as it became the safest of havens. From the 1940s on, the beach offered swimming lessons, taught by such stalwarts as Bob Clare, the unforgettable "Bertie" Hendrickson, and Faith McLaughlin. Their moms gathered on the beach blankets to share the latest Farms news. West Beach membership had become a privilege to be envied.

The Misery Island Connection

During the period from 1900-1917, West Beach was the setting off point for a very active summer community on Misery Island. As we have seen, the pier at West Beach was constructed in 1900, the same year that a syndicate of investors launched what they hoped would be a lucrative summer resort on the 89-acre island situated just over half a mile off the Beverly Farms shoreline. Baker's Island, Misery and its small companion Little Misery were part of the original town of Salem. When Beverly was set off in 1668, the islands did not go to the new town, and have always remained in Salem's domain. The island name goes back to the 17th century, when it was known both as "Moulton's Misery" or "Morton's Misery," apparently for the survivor of a long-forgotten shipwreck. For many years it was owned by the Neville family, until the turn to the 20th century, when Annie Neville sold it for the staggering sum of $60,000. The Nov. 29, 1899 edition of the *Salem Evening News* trumpeted this headline "Great Misery Sold To New York Capitalists," with a drop head adding: "Big Modern Hotel Will Be Built, and Great Sum Spent On Improvements." The "New York capitalists" turned out to be a group of Boston investors, who formed the Misery Island Syndicate. But they were as good as their word, and by the next summer had built a clubhouse and nine-hole golf course on the island. Needing a dock at West Beach, it's likely they approached the corporation and helped to foot the bill for the pier that went up the same year.

A definitive history of Misery Island was written by Dr. Reed Harwood, M.D., and published in the EIHC, Vol. 103, 1967. As a child, Reed Harwood enjoyed carefree summers on Misery with his family at his parents' cottage, known as 'Bleak House,' located at the southwest tip of the island. In 1916, when the future doctor was nine, Europe was deep at war, with British and French allied soldiers dying by the thousands in desperate battles with German troops in the trenches of France while the United States continued to profess neutrality. A year later, America's innocence would be over and the first of our "doughboys" were shipping out under General "Black Jack" Pershing to join the fight. Here is how Dr. Harwood began his account of that magical summer when he was a free-spirited 9-year-old:

> In June 1916, we were returning to Misery Island for our sixth consecutive summer. As usual, my brothers and I, on arriving at West Beach, jumped from the car and ran excitedly the length of the pier and down to the float where Captain Johnson was waiting for us with the launch. For the three of us, this was always a moment crowded with pleasurable sensations – the sound of the gentle waves lapping the sands of West Beach, the distinctive seaside aroma of the North Shore, the familiar contours of Misery Island; and above all, the silhouette of our house on the island's western tip, scarcely a mile away across the placid bay.
>
> For myself, I can say truthfully that the excitement and the impatient anticipation I felt that day on the West Beach pier had the quality of romantic love. In my eyes (I was almost nine years old), Misery Island was beautiful, and our house, which my parents tongue in cheek had named 'Bleak House,' was the perfect summer home.

Half a century later, that wonderful boyhood memory of arriving at West Beach was still evergreen. But by the time Reed entered his teens, Misery would be deserted by all of its summer folk except a caretaker.

The Misery Island Club constructed, in addition to the clubhouse and golf course, a water tower, a tennis court, and an annex (unfinished). The clubhouse would have several names over the years, including the Casino (an unfortunate choice) and even one year the "Beverly Farms Hotel," as a tribute to the launching site even though all property on the island was taxed by Salem. Godfrey Lowell Cabot of Beverly Farms, a pioneer promoter of aviation before World War I, built an airplane hangar on the island about 1915 to house his hydroplane, on which he practiced water landings and takeoffs along with experiments on refueling planes in flight.. There were also several privately owned summer cottages on Great Misery, whose occupants also used West Beach for their jumping off point. An islander who wanted to go to Boston for a day's office work could easily take the launch to West Beach, walk to the Beverly Farms depot to catch the train, then do the same thing in reverse that afternoon. In 1901, the Harvard classes of 1886 and 1891 held their June class reunions at Misery Island, complete with brass band, which must have occasioned much excitement in the Farms with all the going and coming.

But the original Misery Island Syndicate was founded on a house of cards, and was quickly doomed to failure. Dr. Harwood reported that membership in the Misery Island Club cost $25 a season in 1901, with a limit of 350 members, meaning that the syndicate was going to finance a $100,000 construction debt with an annual income of $8,750 in dues, plus whatever concession profits could be generated. The shaky Misery Island Syndicate soon collapsed in a foreclosure sale, but was replaced in 1904 by the Misery Island Trust. That operation was much more successful, and ran things for more than a decade. To generate additional revenue, the trust sold a half dozen building lots on the island to private owners, including the Harwoods (in 1909), who built summer cottages and added a short-lived sense of permanence to the island colony. In addition to the Casino buildings, dock and Mr. Cabot's hangar, the island boasted a barn (which Dr. Harwood estimated had been standing for a century,) a water tower supplied by a gasoline pump, an apple orchard planted by a former island tenant, a well, a small fresh water pond, and a caretaker's cottage. The caretaker who operated the steam launch had a scow on which he could tow supplies. A single telephone line strung beneath the sea provided communications with the mainland.

However, after a prosperous decade, things began to unravel on Misery. Late in 1915, the trust mortgaged its property to the Naumkeag Trust Co. of Salem to pay off debts. That was the beginning of the end. In February of 1917, the trust sold all but the 12 privately owned acres on the island to what was called the "Mystery Island Company." Obviously, the new owners took a dislike to the island's name, and sought to make it something more attractive. But the Mystery Island promoters faced a triple whammy – the silliness of the name, restrictions imposed by a nation at war, and most importantly, failure to attract enough investors to finance the operation. As a result, they never opened for business in 1918. The property was foreclosed again and sold at auction for a mere $2,500 in November of 1918, as the Armistice was ending World War I. (EIHC, Vol. CIII, p. 215).

The demise of the Casino proved to be the death of the island as a summer resort, even chasing away the private cottage owners. The closing, in Reed Harwood's words, "robbed the island of much of its charm," and most of the summer residents did not return to their cottages in 1919, even though the world was again at peace.

The Harwood family continued to summer at Bleak House through 1920, when they were the last island residents except for the caretaker employed to keep trespassers away. Connolly Brothers, the Beverly Farms contracting firm, leased part of the island for a few years. Then in May of 1926 a blaze, supposedly started when a trash fire got out of hand, swept the middle of the island and destroyed the deserted casino buildings.

The most serious threat to Misery occurred in 1935 when Coastal Oils Terminal of Beverly, eying the island for offloading and storage of fuel, obtained an option to buy the property of the defunct Mystery Island Company, and asked the Salem City Council to permit tanks for storing twelve million gallons. That certainly aroused the local citizenry. An association was formed which raised money to buy all of the island except for the 12 privately owned acres, and deeded it over to the Trustees of Reservations for permanent protection from development. The Beverly-based Trustees later raised sufficient funds to purchase the last privately held parcels. The great New England Hurricane of 1938 destroyed the dock at the end of the West Beach pier, but it was no great loss since it was no longer needed.

As for Bleak House, in 1933 Dr. Harwood's father succeeded in selling the now derelict cottage for $1,000. One of the authors recalls as a small boy in 1946, walking the sands as far as Prides Beach in search of sand dollars (we knew better than to venture onto Eleo Sears's beachfront), looking out at the island and seeing Bleak House at the rocky far tip. By then it seemed to be the only building still standing on Misery, although Godfrey Cabot's hangar might have survived. The name Bleak House somehow seemed appropriate for such a lonely yet fascinating (from a distance) place. Then, late on Halloween night in 1946, vandals who must have sneaked out to the island by boat set Bleak House on fire.

Former Beverly Deputy Fire Chief Bob May compiled a log of all major fire events in Beverly from the 18th century on, a copy of which is on file at the Historical Society. Although Misery Island belongs to Salem, persons who spotted the flames also called the Beverly Fire Department, as appears from the following log item: "Misery Island – House, Nov. 1, 1946, Fri., 12:28 a.m." Obviously, there was nothing the Fire Department could do. The next day, nothing could be seen of the Harwoods' one time place of joyful summers except the foundation pillars, some of which are still discernible from the shore.

With the opening of the grand pavilion, backed by the satellite "small bathhouse," the West Beach Corporation entered a tranquil period when hot fun in the summertime was the name of the game. There must, of course, have been some spats among the Board of Directors, and occasional complaints from members regarding enforcement of rules or beach cleanliness, but all in all things went smoothly. The superintendent and his seasonal beach crew took care of raking seaweed, keeping the buildings clean and seeing to orderly operations. In 1936 a matron was added to the summer staff. The beach store at the west end of the pavilion was leased by the corporation to a seasonal operator, so beach-goers could purchase food and sundries. In 1939, Miss Mary F. Malone was proprietor of the West Beach Store at 131 West St., described in the city directory as a "refreshment shop." But all good things must come to an end, and at West Beach that happened with shocking suddenness.

The morning of Thursday, July 15, 1948, dawned bright and clear and with the promise of hot mid-summer weather, a perfect beach day for those who didn't have to work. Some Beverly Farms folks were planning to omit the beach in favor of taking the train to Boston to watch the Red Sox play the Detroit Tigers in an afternoon game at Fenway Park. Even though the Sox were in a hot pennant race and ended up in a first place tie with Cleveland (Manager Joe McCarthy would brcak New England hearts by starting washed-up reliever Denny Galehouse in the one-game playoff instead of rookie sensation Mel Parnell; old Joe just didn't trust rookies in big games); it was possible back then to get good seats for a weekday afternoon contest on game day. Some Farms people did go to Fenway to take their minds off a disaster back home, and were among the 14,403 fans who saw the Sox trounce the Tigers, 13-5, behind right-hand pitcher Jack Kramer.

Most railroad crossings on the Gloucester Branch would get automatic gates in 1949, but in '48 they still were minded by crossing tenders stationed in track-side shanties, who cranked down the gates by hand as a train approached. Lewis Grant of Gloucester was the gate-tender assigned to the day shift at Lee's Crossing, near the lower intersection of West and Hale streets. He arrived for work as usual on the morning of July 15 at about 5:45 a.m., in plenty of time to check things over before the arrival of the first train from Rockport to Boston, number 2500. Although the first diesel to run on the branch, one of the odd-ball BL-2s, made a few Sunday appearances that summer, the P-2 Pacific steamers still handled nearly all of the passenger trains. Grant heard a strange crackling noise. At first he thought it might be coming from the roadbed, since in hot weather the fish plates that held the rails to the crossties sometimes were said to expand audibly. Then he looked up and saw the cloud of smoke rising from the direction of nearby West Beach. He ran to the fire alarm box located on Hale Street just a few yards away from his shanty, and pulled the hook.

Back in the days before establishment of a fire alarm office at Beverly's Central Station, one firefighter was assigned to the alarm desk on the overnight shift. At 5:49 a.m., the alarm system clattered into operation as Box 643–Lee's Crossing–punched out on the tape. The watchman alerted the Beverly Farms station and the crew of Engine 8 at Central, which in those days responded to every alarm box in the city. At about the same time, a motorist who had spotted the smoke drove to the fire station on West Street, leaning on the horn. First on the fire scene were Ladder 2 and Engine 3, the memorable 1925 Ahrens-Fox pumper with its huge silvered pressure dome. Engine 3 was 23 years old and rather obsolete, with its steering wheel on the right hand side and mechanical brakes. It had taken quite a beating at the massive woods fire in the Farms the previous October, but it had been the latest and best when it was new, and it still could pump hard when called upon. No amount of water could have quelled that blaze, because the grand West Beach pavilion was burning from end to end. Deputy Chief Leo J. Murphy ordered a second alarm, but nothing could be done to save what Hardy & Day had built 37 years before.

As Box 643 blared out four times over the horn atop the station in the Square to alert the call firefighters who in those days backed up the full-timers, Beverly Farms residents awakened to an unpleasant surprise. The direction of the huge black cloud that was rising in the sky could only mean either that one of the large waterfront estates was ablaze, or it was the bathhouse. A crowd quickly gathered and watched in silence as flames tore through the pavilion. The heat could be felt 100 yards away. There were at that time no houses across the street from the beach. The best the firefighters could do was to keep the blaze from spreading to the small bathhouse and to the nearby wooden pier. Yeoman work was done by Edgar Kirby and Morgan Cole as they fought the heat to man the powerful deck gun on Engine 48, a 1933 vehicle which the Beverly department had acquired as war surplus just one month before. The roof soon collapsed in a storm of sparks, but it would be hours until the whole thing was reduced to a pile of rubble. The fire was initially termed "suspicious," because midnight shift policeman James Mood said he had checked the premises between 3 and 3:30 a.m., finding everything in order. Eventually it came to be believed that someone using a grill on the beach the previous evening might have put it away in a locker while still too warm, causing a smoldering fire that eventually caught in the tinder dry wood and quickly spread.

One of the authors, a child at the time, remembers hearing an adult friend lament, "We've lost our beach!" That seemed a bit drastic to a child; after all, the sand was still there and the ocean was still there. But loss of the pavilion at the height of the beach season was a massive blow to the West Beach Corporation. Not only were office, store, lockers, toilets, showers and beach cleaning tools gone, the huge pile of debris posed a considerable hazard to anyone accessing the beach property. Horace J. H. Sears, a Hillcrest Road resident, was then president of West Beach. He and his board of directors met in emergency session to decide what to do next. First on the agenda was to clean up the mess. Beverly Farms residents rolled up their sleeves and pitched in. Quick to volunteer were the many World War II veterans who belonged to Michael J. Cadigan Post 46 of the American Legion, the local Boy Scouts, and the players on the two baseball teams in the Farms – the adult team sponsored by Post 46, and the teen-age team known as the Beverly Farms Indians. Women volunteered for the duty of policing the beach property to keep children safe during the emergency. The Capaldi Bros. construction firm sent in some heavy equipment, and the Fire Department gave the beach a big boost by permitting the flammable debris to be burned on the premises, saving the cost of trucking it off to the dump. Once the debris was cleared after a few days, the pavilion site was graded, both to keep curious children safe and to allow for additional parking. Those who had rented lockers were told they now had no choice other than to change at home, unless, of course, they were lucky enough to have lockers in the small bathhouse. (Some of those people agreed to share with less fortunate friends.) The directors quickly moved to erect temporary bathroom facilities for the remainder of the summer season.

Loss of the pavilion was estimated at $80,000, which would be ten times more in today's money. That figure did not, of course, include the private contents of lockers, and for many people this posed a major problem. It might have still been the height of summer, but replacing lost beach gear wasn't easy. We well remember going with one dear lady as she shopped to replace her bathing suit which had been lost in the fire, and which had been her favorite. Visits to three department or clothing stores produced the same result. It was mid-July, and the stores were already stocked with fall fashions. Inquiries to clerks produced an incredulous reply: "One-piece bathing suits? We don't stock bathing suits now! You have to buy those in the spring." Finally, in the fourth store, a sympathetic clerk allowed as how there might still be a few women's bathing suits in the back store room. The clerk emerged a few minutes later, four or five one-piece women's bathing suits draped over one arm; they were leftovers available on discount. Only one was in the lady's size. She didn't particularly care for the style and she hated the color, but realizing there was no alternative if she wanted to patronize the beach for the last six weeks of the season, she paid the discount price and considered herself fortunate.

It also was fortunate that the West Beach Corporation held an insurance policy on the lost pavilion, although it wouldn't cover the full replacement cost. President Sears, while thanking everyone for their patience and assistance, pledged that the beach would do its best to be up and running at full throttle in time for the 1949 season. Plans began to take shape to replace the lost pavilion with a new concrete block structure which would have lockers, showers, store, restrooms, first aid room, long covered veranda, tide and temperature board, all the necessary amenities that had been lost. But recovery wouldn't be instantaneous, and the beach would have to struggle through another makeshift summer until everything was back to normal. The May 21, 1949 edition of the *Beverly Evening Times* had a front page story headlined: "Construction of new West Beach bathhouse may get underway within 2 weeks." The story reported that the architectural firm Fitzpatrick & Lunt, engaged by the West Beach board, had designed a "semi-fireproof" structure which would include a roofed veranda 95 feet long and 13 feet deep. The number of lockers would be cut by more than half to 106, due to lack of funds. Because of the cut in the number of locker rooms, the West Beach directors decreed that from now on, two families would have to share one. Writing in his Beverly Farms column on June 6, Joseph M. Donovan (he was newsman, alderman, Legion post commander and for years "Uncle Sam" in the July 4 parade) reported that work on the new beach building was "progressing rapidly." The firm of Conie & Donahue had been awarded the construction contract, and began work 12 hours after winning the bid for a sum that was not reported. While the job would not of course be done in time for the opening of the beach, it was hoped the bathhouse would be ready for use before the end of the season. Meanwhile, parking stickers could be obtained from treasurer Gerard J. Deeley. A follow-up report on June 21 noted that Farms residents were pleased with the progress of the job. But since the cost would be more than the funds available, the Corporation would be launching a drive for contributions from the membership to help make up the difference. The new building certainly lacked the rustic charm of its predecessor and there was no high lookout for children to climb to. But the new bathhouse was safer, and it has stood up well over 65 years of service. West Beach had survived a major disaster, and entered the 1950s in solid condition.

Disaster number two would strike 30 years later, not in the form of fire but of storm. It was a blizzard against which all future winter storms would be measured, the infamous "Blizzard of '78."

On the morning of Monday, Feb. 6, 1978, all of the forecasters agreed that greater Boston was in for a storm. The "official" Weather Service prediction was that snow would begin in the Boston area around noon, and would accumulate 6 to 10 inches before ending Tuesday morning. Schools would open Monday, and at least the morning commute would be uneventful. Residents sighed but decided they could cope; after all, just a little more than two weeks before, on Jan. 20, the "storm of the century" had shattered 90-year-old records for the most accumulation in one day. The new record would last a little over two weeks, and nobody remembers the January storm. Some private forecasters thought the initial predictions weren't to be believed. One of those was Elliott Abrams, head of the New Jersey-based Accu-Weather, which at that time was contracted by the former Boston radio station WHDH. At 5:30 a.m. Abrams told listeners to the popular "Jess Cain Show" to expect 10 to 14 inches, "and it might be quite a bit more." He also injected a chilling warning: "Don't take this one lightly, folks. This is a dangerous storm." By noon, although it wasn't snowing, it was obvious we were in for it, very soon. Gov. Michael S. Dukakis urged employers to let their workers leave early. Those who did get on the road by 4 p.m., especially if they were going north from Boston, would make it safely. But those who waited longer would find themselves trapped on Route 128 and other major highways as the storm struck with a fury that no plows or drivers could cope with. Hurricane force winds whipped up monstrous coastal tides. The crew of the Gloucester pilot boat "Can Do" would perish when the boat sank south of Misery Island while trying to go to the aid of a Coast Guard craft that became lost after its radar went out as it was answering the distress call of a tanker dragging its anchor in Salem Harbor. (The Coast Guardsmen eventually spotted a shore beacon and made it safely to the Jubilee Yacht Club pier.) The storm continued unabated until early Tuesday evening, producing a state of emergency that would continue for the rest of the week. The 8 p.m. train from Boston Monday night was the last that would get through to Rockport, as the record tide undermined the tracks between West Beach and West Manchester. No trains would run for a week, until repairs could be made. After a test train went through the following Sunday, the first train operated Monday. Fortunately for the people of Beverly Farms, most of them did not lose power despite the potent winds and massive amounts of drifting snow.

But when the storm finally abated and people got a look at the shoreline, they were in for a shock. The West Beach bathhouses had survived the pounding, but the pier was gone – not damaged--it had completely disappeared. Only a few stubs of the shoreline end pilings could be seen to show that a pier had ever existed. Normally, Lee's Rocks at the east end of the corporation bounds, along with Cove Rocks, provided a bit of shelter to the corporation property. But in this diabolical storm, the central force concentrated on the 78-year-old pier, not only ripping up the deck but tearing away the pilings as though they were straw men. Adding to the stunning sight was the fact that less than 200 yards to the west, the remains of a decrepit private pier appeared to be untouched.. Pieces of the West Beach pier would wash ashore over the next few days.

There was nothing the Corporation could do. Had the pier been merely damaged, it could, of course, have been repaired if the Corporation could afford to do so. But as it was gone, any effort at replacement meant starting from scratch. The welter of state and federal permits required to build a new pier stopped any attempt to rebuild, even if funds were available – an unlikely possibility. A suggestion that the Corporation might apply for state or federal grants was quickly dismissed, since it was realized that accepting even a dollar of grant money would have forced the Corporation to open the premises to the public. The pier that had been the pride of West Beach was gone forever. As a stop-gap, the directors decided to purchase a large float that could be moored off shore as a diving platform. This was used for several years, but once the float (which had to be hauled out and stored in the off-season at considerable expense) began to wear out, it was decided not to replace it. Beach-goers too young to remember the stately pier can't imagine how much others miss it. Those were the two major disasters in the history of the West Beach Corporation. There have been other sad moments.

Esther Liley, longtime matron, died suddenly just as the beach was about to open for the 1960 season. And in 2003, popular West Beach president and man-about-the Farms Ralph Coluntino passed away at the beginning of another beach season; he was remembered at a memorial celebration where he most wanted – West Beach.

Celebrating the Fourth of July

No introspective about West Beach and the West Beach Corporation could be complete without mentioning the important role the beach has played for more than a century of Beverly Farms Fourth of July celebrations. There is a public misconception that the beach sponsors the holiday events, including the fireworks display that traditionally caps off the night of the Fourth. Actually, the beach is simply the locale. All holiday activities are organized and paid for by the volunteer Farms/Prides Fourth of July Committee, which makes the plans and raises the funds to cover all the expenses that seem to get higher every year. But because the stretch of beach and the bathhouse facilities is the natural center of attraction for the day, and the only place in the Farms where a safe fireworks display is possible, the Corporation has for over 100 years made its premises available to the committee.

The day is intended for Beverly Farms residents, West Beach subscribers and their families, but traditionally the property becomes host to non-members, especially for the fireworks. That show also attracts a fleet of boat-owners who moor their craft between the beach and Misery Island to enjoy an aerial display that is considered one of the best in the area. When possible, committee members take a boat out to collect contributions – sometimes given freely and sometimes refused.

For many years the public was welcome for the fireworks. Later, attempts were made to limit admission to Farms residents who had purchased tickets. In recent years, as expenses continued to rise, admission tickets have been sold to anyone willing to pay, but parking at the beach is still restricted to those with stickers. It has become standard for the police to shut down all streets in the area at 7 p.m. on the Fourth to improve public safety.

A "traditional" Fourth in the Farms starts out with the Horribles Parade which forms up on Oak Street near the railroad station and steps off at 8 a.m. for Henry J. Dix Park (first known as the Beverly Farms Playground and renamed in 1944 for a Farms Marine who gave his life for his country in World War II. At times over the years a ball game has followed at the park. Then in the afternoon the action shifts to West Beach, the scene of games and races for children as well as family picnics. A band concert on the beach veranda in the early evening is then followed by the fireworks.

But despite the perception of tradition, there have been years when things were different. World Wars I and II put a decided damper on the celebration. And over the last 60 years there have been at least two times when there were no fireworks – once for reasons not remembered (money, perhaps) and once when concerns over liability insurance for the West Beach Corporation after an incident the year before led to cancellation.

The fireworks got their start at the beginning of the 20th century with the construction of the West Beach pier. That structure made it possible for aerial displays to be shot off, and the "set pieces," colorful pinwheels and 'waterfalls' attached to wooden frames, to be erected. The loss of the pier changed things dramatically. Now the only choice is for the Fourth of July Committee to rent a barge from which the aerial display (no more set pieces) can be fired off.

1898 – The holiday on the North Shore was marred by the "Surf City" disaster. While on a pleasure cruise in the Salem-Beverly harbor, the steam boat foundered in a sudden squall. Eight persons drowned, but many other passengers and crew members were rescued through the heroism of residents who rushed to the scene aboard anything that could float.

In Beverly Farms, a "great and glorious Fourth" was celebrated with West Beach, which had by then evolved into a recreation spot, as the center. People brought picnic lunches to the seashore, and it was, in the words of the *Beverly Times* reporter, "one big family party." In the evening, the "long row of bathhouses" (those were, of course, the beach shacks erected by the Publicover Bros.) were decorated with lanterns. In what would be a preview of fireworks displays to come, at dusk the picnickers set off firecrackers they had brought for the occasion, and topped everything off by sending up colored lights on balloons.

1908 – The newspaper commented on a "splendid program at the Farms." The Horribles Parade had yet to come into existence, but the day's activities started with two baseball games at "Marshall's Field," one for the boys at 8:30 a.m., another for the men an hour later. Then everything moved to West Beach. The afternoon's highlight was a race, but not for kids. It was a one-half mile horse race along both the Corporation and private stretches of sand. Anybody who owned a horse they considered fast could enter, with all to carry 143 pounds. (We don't know who won.) There was of course no pavilion veranda yet, but early in the evening the Rowley Brass Band found space to entertain everyone with a concert of patriotic and marching music. This was followed by a "grand illumination" of the beach, a soon to be traditional line of ignited railroad flares. And now that the pier had been in place for several years, a fireworks display had become the awaited conclusion of the day's events. Edwin F. Campbell was chairman of the Fourth of July Committee that year.

1918 – With the world at war and many of the community's younger residents either fighting in France or training at state-side military camps, the Beverly Farms correspondent for the *Times* reported that the "Fourth passed off very quietly. No sports or amusements of any kind were scheduled." The only public activity held to mark Independence Day was a concert by the United Shoe Machinery Co. Band, which performed between 2 and 3 p.m. on the veranda of the West Beach pavilion, built seven years before.

1928 – That year featured a more traditional celebration of the holiday, although there still was no mention of a parade. A baseball game in the morning was something of a pickup affair – married men vs. single men. In the afternoon at West Beach there were children's games along with a special treat, a Punch and Judy puppet show. The Beverly Cadet Band performed in the afternoon, and following a refreshment break the band members took to the pavilion again for an evening concert to put the crowd in the mood for a "fine display" of fireworks. Beverly had its own fireworks display, at Lyons Park/Dane Street Beach.

1938 – With the Fourth on a Monday, the Farms turned the holiday weekend into a three-day celebration. On Saturday evening at the library hall, children were treated to free "talkies" (still the term for sound motion pictures which had been around for a decade or so, and probably in this case featured cartoons). Sunday afternoon at the Farms Park (now Dix Park) there was both a baseball game between the Beverly Farms Athletic Club and the Boston & Maine Railroad Athletic Club, and a tennis tournament on the park's recently constructed courts. On the holiday morning, the now traditional Horribles Parade started at 8 a..m. from the depot. The Farms A.C. took the field for the second time in as many days to play the 400 Club. Then it was off to West beach for everyone, with a band concert at 1:30, sports and games for boys and girls starting at 2, with another concert at 7 topped off by the "illumination" at 9 and of course the fireworks.

World War II would soon intervene, and from 1942-45 the needs of the military meant that no gunpowder was available for fireworks. With everyone's eyes on foreign battle scenes and thoughts on residents far from home, there was little appetite for celebration. Rationing, especially of gasoline, kept everybody close to home. In 1944, for example, no parade or much of anything else was planned on what would be a "quiet Fourth." However, the West Beach Corporation did what it could to brighten the holiday, throwing open its gates to the general public of Beverly and presenting a musical program of patriotic tunes on the beach pavilion in the afternoon.

1948 – Just 11 days before the disastrous fire, the Farms Fourth of July celebrants would make use of their much loved Hardy & Day-built beach pavilion for the last time. After the Horribles Parade and a regular Beverly Twi-League ball game at Dix Park between the Cadigan Post team of Beverly Farms and the Beverly Youth Association club, also known as the Beverly Town Team (won by the Farms, 4-0), action as usual shifted to West Beach for children's races and a pair of band concerts, at 2 and 7. The fireworks that night were said to have cost $1,000. Arthur Sheehan was the committee chairman.

1958 – The Horribles Parade was held as usual, but instead of a baseball game, a drum corps exhibition provided the post-parade entertainment. Again, band concerts on the new bathhouse veranda were held at 1 and 7, with fireworks at 9. The Ryal Side neighborhood held its own fireworks show at Obear Park. The West Beach work crew watched the Farms display from the roof of the new bathhouse.

1968 – This was a strange holiday in some ways. A headline in the Times blared: "Farms Fourth Not Like Old Days." The Horribles Parade was said to have been a bust, with only five floats entered instead of the usual 15 or 20, and the post parade crowd at Dix Park was smaller than usual. The baseball game was a Little League contest. At West Beach, the Huntsmen Band of Hamilton played a single concert in the afternoon, and the games featured the running of the Joseph M. Donovan Memorial "marathon" along the wet sand to Prides and back. Evening activities at West Beach were restricted to a "family entertainment" at 6:30, featuring an appearance by Boston children's

television personality Rex Trailer. There was no mention of fireworks that year, which may have contributed to the "not like old days" spirit.

1978 – Fireworks were at the heart of the day's events at West Beach, but with a big difference. Destruction of the pier in the February 6-7 blizzard meant that the only way to have a display at the beach was for the Fourth of July Committee to rent a barge for use of the fireworks company crew and moor it off shore. This greatly added to the expense of the show, but the committee decided it was worth it.

Surviving a Bitter Challenge

For 140 years after its incorporation, the West Beach association faced no threats to its standing as a private, non-profit corporation. It overcame its first significant hurdle in the 1990s, when the City of Beverly, in a challenge to the tax exempt status of the beach, issued a tax bill for the full assessed value of the property. The corporation had no choice other than to pay while disputing the change. The battle to regain tax exempt status was successful, but the corporation, in a spirit of compromise, agreed to make an annual payment to the city in lieu of taxes.

Far more serious, and threatening, were the events of 1998-2001, when some disgruntled Beverly residents, for reasons of their own, banded together in an all-out assault on West Beach. Their stated goal was for the city of take control of the beach property and open it to the public. This group and its leaders decided to go after the 1852 legislation on the grounds that the people of Beverly had been "victims of a scheme that quickly changed an innocent sounding petition into a special act of the legislature. The result is that the people of Beverly unwittingly voted away their traditional use of the finest beach in Beverly." (Allen Hovey). Another accusation was that the incorporation of West Beach in 1852 was "rife with omissions, misstatements and either gross ineptitude or outright fraud at several key points in the process," and that "to accomplish all of this in less than three months in 1852 was amazing and attests to the political power of the vested interests behind the process." (Hovey). By calling it "a piece of classist legislation," the critical implication was clear that wealthy and influential Beverly Farms residents had connived to steal a valuable public resource for their own benefit.

Hovey, in his analysis "Beverly's West Beach and the West Beach Corporation," concisely demolishes those claims. He wrote: "The phrase 'victims of a scheme' is a terrible accusation to make against the citizens of the Town of Beverly in 1852." Charging that the process was carried out in less than three months, wrote Hovey, "fully misrepresents the historical facts." He added: "In truth, the historical process began in May, 1851, took 14 months to incorporate the West

Beach Corporation, and is a uniquely interesting example of the workings of the will of the people through town government in 19th century Massachusetts."

The residents of Beverly Farms, having experienced disputes over rights to harvest seaweed at the beach, took the matter to the Beverly selectmen and through them to the warrant for the June 7, 1851, special town meeting.. That meeting, at which all Beverly voters were eligible to participate, agreed to refer the article back to the Board of Selectmen. That elected board, researching the original award of the beach to John West, a grant never rescinded, came up with what they thought was the most equitable solution. They advised the men of Beverly Farms to organize themselves into a body for the purpose of petitioning the state legislature for an act of incorporation. There never was an indication that any "rights" of the public were being given away. With official approval, the men of the Farms followed suit with a petition to the General Court in October, and they were rewarded with the signing of Chapter 157 on April 28, 1852. Before that was done, the citizens of Beverly had to ratify the act again at their annual town meeting in March of 1852, with the added amendment that the new corporation continue the original charge to John West in 1666 – that of maintaining the causeway and roadway abutting the beach premises. That remained in effect until the designation of the street as a state highway, at which time the Commonwealth assumed responsibility of all aspects of the road. Any Beverly resident who might have felt aggrieved at the change to what had for nearly two centuries been considered private property could have raised objections at either town meeting, at the public meeting of the selectmen, or before either the House of Representatives or state Senate. Since there is no record that anybody ever did so, there seems to be no justification for claiming that any "gross ineptitude or outright fraud" could have occurred. There were a lot of smart people in the town of Beverly in the mid-19th century, and to think that none of them would have seen through a "fraud" beggars belief. The selectmen, being answerable to the entire town, would have had to answer for it had they been parties to a fraud. The process was completed in July 1852 with the election of officers and adoption of corporation bylaws, again with no objection from anyone in Beverly.

One argument advanced to "prove" that Beverly residents had enjoyed free access to West Beach was that the famous author-poet Lucy Larcom, who was born in 1824 and grew up on what is now Wallis Street in downtown Beverly before her father died and her mother moved the family to Lowell, had visited West Beach as a child. Of course she did. Lucy's uncle and aunt, David and Betsey Larcom, lived in the Farms at what is now part of the property of St. John's Church at 705 Hale St. In those safer days when children in their limited play time were allowed to roam more freely, Lucy and her brother John thought nothing of walking four miles to visit their aunt and uncle. They knew some of the village children. In the late 1820s there was no gate guardian at the beach, and even if there were, who would have objected to children going there to play?

Hovey (a Rockport resident with no inherent interest in the beach) also takes pains to point out that the 102 men of Beverly Farms who signed the petition were anything but a collection of the rich and famous with lots of political pull. They were, he wrote, "farmers, mariners and people of the working class of Beverly, not an elitist upper class of wealthy folks." He cites the 1850 census, in which Peter Pride, the first to sign the petition, was a farmer, and his son Peter Jr., the seventh signer, was a 26-year-old shoemaker. West D. Eldridge, the second signer, was a farmer like the senior Pride, and his son Stephen, 24, was a mariner. Later in the 19th century there would indeed be wealthy residents of Beverly Farms (at least in the summer), but those people had no need for West Beach. He also noted that West Beach, with its 650 feet of shoreline and limited parking, is small in comparison with Beverly's public Dane Street Beach. And the remaining 3,400 feet of what shows on some maps as West Beach is privately held through registered deeds. In Hovey's words, "After reviewing the facts, it should be clear that the case against the existence of the West Beach Corporation...is totally without merit. And likewise, talk about using a revised Beverly Charter to rewrite Beverly's history and set the stage for a very ugly civil war between the people of Beverly Farms and their fellow citizens in Beverly's other five Wards will be extremely divisive for the community-at-large, and, in the end, will in all likelihood be a total waste of time and energy." His prediction was right on target.

But the anti-West Beach people forged ahead. In July 1999 they filed a petition seeking an amendment to the Beverly City Charter that would allow for opening the beach to the public. Their claim was that Chapter 157 of the Acts of 1852 was a "Special Law" that had, in effect, created a quasi-public and not a private corporation. The matter would go before the voters in the municipal election of November 1999, with both a question authorizing the creation of a Charter Commission charged with looking into the West Beach matter and, assuming the question would pass, elect nine members to serve on that commission. Playing on latent anti-Beverly Farms "snob" sentiment among some Beverly residents, along with the "carrot" that everyone soon would be able to utilize West Beach, it was no surprise that the charter commission advocates succeeded in getting their question passed. And since members of the group of petitioners won six of the nine seats on the commission, they would prevail through the process over the next 18 months. The West Beach board did not take this lying down, of course. Through the efforts of its legal team, headed by Attorney Thomas Fallon, the corporation fought back hard. One argument used was that any attempt to "open" West Beach would in effect be a land-taking, leaving the city liable to pay the owners, in this case the people of Beverly Farms, the full value of the property. The Charter Commission majority rebuffed any attempt to include discussion of any other aspects of Beverly's Charter; their only concern was West Beach.

In February of 2001 a preliminary report of the commission was forwarded to State Attorney General Thomas Reilly, and the opinion of the top state legal official was the first of three major victories for the West Beach Corporation. Reilly's advice was that the proposed takeover was "inconsistent with the Constitution and laws of the Commonwealth." He ruled that Chapter 157 was not a "Special Law" under the Home Rule Amendment, and therefore not susceptible to charter amendment. Despite this, the Charter Commission voted 6-3 in April to place on the ballot for the city's 2001 election a question to open West Beach to the public. Instead of dissolving the existing corporation, the proposal would create a new board of directors which would be elected on a city-wide ballot, guaranteeing that Beverly Farms residents, comprising only one voting precinct out of 12, would have no say in the running of the beach.

A minority report was filed by the three dissenting members of the commission. In addition to placing the question on the ballot, the Charter Commission insisted that both the majority and minority reports be printed and distributed to all registered voter households. It could set the stage for one of the ugliest episodes in Beverly history, one certain to leave a lasting legacy of bitter feelings. At that point the Beverly City Council courageously stepped in to put a stop to the nonsense. At a meeting in May, the Council voted not to allow the question to be placed on the November ballot. The elected body also said no to the expense of printing and distributing the Charter Commission's final and minority reports. Furious, the commission majority and other plaintiffs (14 in all) then filed suit in Superior Court, seeking a declaratory judgment that would force the City Council to comply with the commission mandate to place the matter before the voters. The West Beach Corporation was included as a defendant. At that time several property owners in the vicinity of the beach ("West Beach Neighbors") were allowed to enter the case as co-defendants. They were concerned that opening West Beach to the public would subject them to damage because the inevitable spillover from the limited corporation property would directly and adversely impact them.

The case went before the Honorable Nancy Merrick, justice of the Superior Court, and was heard at the courthouse in Salem. On Oct. 10, 2001, Judge Merrick issued the judgment that once and for all put down the attempt to seize West Beach, as she ordered: "...Plaintiffs' motion for summary judgment is DENIED, the defendants Beverly City Council and West Beach Corporation's respective motions for summary judgment are ALLOWED. West Beach neighbors' emergency cross motion...for declaratory relief is hereby ALLOWED." (Judge Merrick's opinion, Superior Court Department of the Trial Court, p. 13.)

In her opinion, Judge Merrick thoroughly reviewed the history of the case and of Chapter 157. She rejected any argument that Chapter 157 was a Special Law, concluding that it had in fact created a private corporation. She ruled that the Charter Commission majority was off-base when it concluded that the conditions placed upon the corporation in 1852 were now relevant, in these words: "The Court does not accept that in doing so the West Beach Corporation was thus transformed into a quasi-municipal entity," and that "the Court is unconvinced that the 'purpose' of the Corporation's founding was maintenance of the causeway and wall."

She also, on page 10 of her opinion, states: "The persons empowered to execute c. 157 are distanced from the governmental authority of Beverly by the express language of the statute. The Legislature spoke only of the 'members' of the corporation, its 'clerk' and 'treasurer.' No method for their selection is articulated, and furthermore no evidence is presented that it was by any other method other than by selection by the self-contained body. Certainly were it otherwise, such as selection by the townspeople, that information would be a critical component of c. 157 and presumably referenced..." On the next page, Judge Merrick writes, "The private act of incorporation creating West Beach Corporation is outside the reach of G.L. c 43B and the Beverly Charter Commission lacks authority under the statute to amend, repeal or in any way alter the status of the West Beach Corporation. To effectuate the change the plaintiffs seek the appropriate recourse is to the Legislature, empowered as it is to take land for the public use and justly compensate the owners." In other words only an eminent domain proceeding could change the beach ownership.

Judge Merrick's ruling was greeted with cheers and relief in Beverly Farms. It had been a long and hard struggle, leaving some bitter feelings in its wake, but the West Beach Corporation had, backed by some important rulings, survived a vindictive attempt to destroy a century and a half of local history.

The West Beach Corporation Today

Although its operations have been "modernized," the West Beach Corporation continues to function in the 21st century in much the same way it did when newly founded in 1852. Voting membership is available to any Beverly Farms resident 18 or older with the payment of a one-time token membership fee

No resident is required to join to be eligible for beach privileges, but only listed members can vote at the annual election. Over the years, that election and the annual meeting have been held on the same evening (once in February, now on the second Thursday in October), but the meeting place has changed – from the Baptist Church (until 1892), then Marshall's Hall at 1 West Street, then the G.A.R. (Grand Army of the Republic) Hall that stood in the Square next to the 1886 fire station, then in the Legion Hall after the G.A.R. faded as the last Civil War veterans died off and the American Legion was born after World War I (that building was torn down in 1956 to make room for the new fire station), then at the Library Hall, and now at Hastings House, the Oak Street headquarters of the Farms/Prides Community Association.

In the early days, meeting notices were posted by the clerk of the corporation at Perry's Corner (Hale and Hart Streets where the store used to be), Asa Ober's corner (now Beverly Farms Square) and at Young's Bend (the sharp curve on upper Hart Street). Now, the clerk mails post cards to all registered members in September. The 2006 card, signed by Clerk Raeann Downey and Vice President Donald MacQuarrie, informed members that nomination papers for president, vice president, clerk, treasurer and directors were to be filed with the clerk or treasurer (Bruce Morris) no later than 5 p.m. Monday, Sept. 25, 2006. To be valid, nomination papers must be signed by at least five members of the corporation. The same notice advised that the annual meeting would be held Thursday, Oct. 12, with polls open from 6:30 to 8:30 p.m., and the business session to follow at 8:30. The original bylaws called for officers to be elected on one piece of paper, and that procedure is still followed. Voters are checked in from the membership list much the same as in any municipal election, and voting booths are set up. The four corporation officers are on the ballot, and the seven candidates who receive the most votes win places on the Board of Directors. The board holds regular meetings to conduct the affairs of the beach, including the hiring of summer staff.

The annual meeting is now held in the library of Hastings House. That event has changed over the years. Back in the 1960s, as many as 50 people might be present at the Library Hall, and the meetings could get a bit rowdy as some people aired gripes or asked loaded questions. Now it is unusual for more than a few members other than the board to hear the reports of the clerk, treasurer and President Steve O'Brien in a session that in 2006 lasted less than 20 minutes. One problem faced by the corporation over the years was that the original boundaries for the membership area became increasingly hard to determine as old landmarks disappeared. After a while it became accepted that the bounds of Ward 6, Precinct 1 constituted Beverly Farms, and persons having proof of residence on streets within the precinct were eligible for parking stickers or walk-in passes. Then in 1971, the corporation moved to establish a new bounds map. One reason for this was the push to "equalize" the voter rolls in all 12 Beverly precincts, with the expectation that Ward 6 would be enlarged. But the corporation had another reason to be concerned. Rumors were rife around the Farms that two large open tracts were being eyed by developers looking to build large, multi-unit apartment complexes. One of those sites was the former Pinanski estate, a sizeable stretch of woodlands on Common Lane just north of Greenwood Avenue. The second source of rumors centered on the rear portion of the former Orchidvale property, where a high-rise development was said to be under discussion. Fortunately, neither of those proposals happened.

But it was a source of worry for the beach directors, since if both developments were to happen they would potentially add up to 200 housing units, swamping a beach that already had far more parking stickers out than it had parking spaces. The solution was to make sure that on the new boundary map, both of the sites in question would be cut out from the membership area. So the western boundary was drawn from Thissell Street to Common Lane, from there along the center of what was then a driveable portion of Greenwood Avenue as far as Webster Avenue, and then cutting across country until joining

Hart Street at what was once called Young's Bend, and on to the Wenham line, taking in Preston Place. That neatly cut out the two rumored development sites. At the time there was only one house in the Farms left outside the boundary, so the residents of that house were specifically given beach privileges.

The beach season begins on Memorial Day weekend and ends on Labor Day. Normally, the premises remain open on the weekend following Labor Day so renters can clean out their lockers before the bathhouse closes for the season. In addition to the happenings on the Fourth of July, a major event that sadly marks the close of summer is a sand castle contest held on the Sunday of Labor Day weekend. Occasionally there are special events to which the public is welcome, such as the annual Ben Bradley Memorial Beach Volleyball Tournament, held on an August day in memory of a popular young Farms resident who died at 19 in a 2001 car crash. A beach superintendent is in charge, and is usually relieved by a night superintendent who takes over at 5 p.m. and remains on duty until the gates are locked at 9.

On most "season" days one of the beach staff is stationed at the gate to check admissions, including persons walking in. On days when the weather is extremely poor, it is common practice to send the beach workers home and not open the bathhouses. At one time one person was hired specifically as a lifeguard, but in recent years the Board of Directors instituted a policy that all candidates for beach helper positions must have Red Cross life-saving certification. Since the demise of the pier, a lifeguard chair is put in place on the sand during the normal beach season.

Stickers are available on two or three Sundays as well as a couple of Wednesday evenings during May and early June. The resident sticker fee currently is $125 for the season, with senior citizens 65-69 paying half price and those over 70 entitled to free admission. Proof of residence is required, and the sticker is placed directly on the car windshield by a member of the board or the superintendent. Stickers may not be transferred. Since more stickers are issued than there are spaces, the rule on parking is "first come, first served." A hot summer weekend day may see a West Beach patron circling the block repeatedly in hopes that someone will have left and freed up a parking spot.

To help out, chalk lines are put down and the staff advises everyone to "park tight." Once the beach closes for the season, the public is welcome within the limits of proper behavior, but restrooms and other facilities are locked up. To save wear and tear and maintenance expense, the upper section of the parking lot is blocked off during the off-season period, and the gates are locked at sunset. At the time a sticker is issued, a list of beach rules is handed out and must be signed. Violators risk the loss of their beach and/or membership privileges until such time as the Board of Directors restores such.

General rules prohibit any activity which disturbs the quiet enjoyment of other patrons. Motor vehicles except for authorized cleanup equipment are barred from the sand. No open fires are allowed at any time, and coals from grills must be extinguished at the water's edge. Glass containers are forbidden for obvious reasons, and loud music is a no-no. Abusive conduct toward any officer, director, employee or patron is punishable by immediate suspension of privileges. Safety rules prohibit rubber tubes or other flotation devices, or the use of spear guns. Ball playing and frisbee throwing are allowed only on the wet sand at low tide, provided the area is not crowded. There are special rules regarding boats, with motors restricted to beyond the swimming area. Row boats registered at the beach office are allowed to be stored along the far wall of the premises near Lee's Rocks. In recent years, the interior of the century-old small bathhouse received a major rebuilding, and the large building was repainted.

One of the quirks of the beach is the "date rock." Back around 1959 a couple of Farms residents (still secret) slipped in one evening and painted the front of the biggest boulder of the Lee's Rocks ledge with the date "1620" in large white numerals, as a takeoff on the famous Plymouth Rock. Actually, they were off by a decade. When the Winthrop Fleet arrived in 1630, a party from the "Arbella" is supposed to have rowed ashore somewhere in the Farms area. But the 1620 rock has become something of a West Beach icon, and ever since someone has renewed the paint every year or two to keep up the tradition.

Finally, there's the sign that stays up for 12 months:

"ABSOLUTELY *NO DOGS YEAR ROUND."*

Appendix: Presidents of the Corporation

Note: a list of the presidents of the West Beach Corporation from 1852 through 1936 was compiled by Elsie Doane. Since the corporation has no central archives, and the whereabouts of records from some of the ensuing years is unknown, it is possible that this list is incomplete. If anyone who served has been left out, we apologize. Of the 24 names known, only one is a woman. The corporation is, in fact, hoping to install a plaque in the bathhouse which will bear the names of all past presidents. We are indebted to Raeann Downey, the present clerk of the corporation, who checked the records back to 1970, which is as far back as her notes go. Raeann provided the names of several presidents in addition to those we previously were sure of. The names of those after Mr. Sears are not necessarily in chronological order.)

WEST BEACH PRESIDENTS, 1852 - 2015

Joseph E. Ober (first president, elected July 12, 1852)
John Knowlton
George Woodbury II
George Pierce
John Woodberry
Nathaniel P. Allen
Daniel W. Hardy
James B. Dow
Frank L. Lomasney
Daniel M. Linehan
Samuel Vaughan
Horace J.H. Sears
Robert Whigham
Robert W. Morris
Ralph Drinkwater
Faith McLaughlin
Joseph Landers
Daniel J. Murphy
F. Wentworth Murray
Douglas Canning
Martin Freeman
Ralph Coluntino (served for 21 years, 1983-2004)
Donald MacQuarrie (acting)*
Stephen O'Brien

*As vice president, Mr. MacQuarrie in 2004 completed the unexpired term after the death of Mr. Coluntino.

www.ingramcontent.com/pod-product-compliance
Ingram Content Group UK Ltd.
Pitfield, Milton Keynes, MK11 3LW, UK
UKHW041916190726
13854UKWH00003B/1277